FARMWORKER'S FRIEND

FARMWORKER'S FRIEND

The Story of Cesar Chavez

David R. Collins

 Carolrhoda Books, Inc./Minneapolis

This book is available in two editions:
Library binding by Carolrhoda Books, Inc.
Soft cover by First Avenue Editions
c/o The Lerner Group
241 First Avenue North, Minneapolis, MN 55401

Library of Congress Cataloging-in-Publication Data

Collins, David R.
  Farmworker's friend : the story of Cesar Chavez / by David R. Collins.
    p. cm.
  Includes bibliographical references and index.
  Summary: Examines the life and accomplishments of the Mexican
American labor activist who helped organize migrant farm workers and
establish a union to fight for their rights.
  ISBN 0-87614-982-4 (lib. bdg.)
  ISBN 1-57505-031-5 (pbk.)
  1. Chavez, Cesar, 1927–   —Juvenile literature. 2. Labor leaders—United
States—Biography—Juvenile literature. 3. Trade-unions—Migrant
agricultural laborers—United States—Officials and employees—
Biography—Juvenile literature. 4. Mexican Americans—Biography—
Juvenile literature. 5. United Farm Workers—History—Juvenile literature.
[1. Chavez, Cesar, 1927– . 2. Labor leaders. 3. Mexican Americans—
Biography. 4. Migrant labor. 5. United Farm Workers.] I. Title.
HD6509.C48C65 1996
331.88'13'092—dc 20
[B]   95-42759

Manufactured in the United States of America
1 2 3 4 5 6 – JR – 01 00 99 98 97 96

CONTENTS

INTRODUCTION

He was not a man you would notice in a crowd. On his tallest day, he stood five feet six inches tall. In his later years, during the early 1990s, he used a cane, propping up a body weakened by a lifetime of picking peas, pulling down walnuts, marching in demonstrations, and fasting. No, Cesar Estrada Chavez did not stand out physically in a crowd. But one-on-one, Cesar showed the spirit that set him apart. For hours he would listen closely to the problems and troubles of other field-workers. They knew and trusted him because he had been a field-worker too. He had stood where they stood, sweating and aching, only to be paid in pennies or a few dollars for a whole day's labor. He understood them, and he knew how to improve their lives.

At a speaker's stand, he could sift through all that he had heard from each person and offer ways of organizing people into action. Cesar Chavez used no fancy words, no eloquent phrases. He did not need to be a polished public speaker. Listeners heard a man share his hopes and dreams for them in a language they knew.

Again and again, Cesar Chavez talked about a union. As important as one person might be, Cesar knew there was greater strength in numbers. Many groups of workers had organized in unions to fight for better working conditions and benefits. Teachers, actors, government and factory employees, and many others had their own unions. Yet there was no union for farmworkers, not the kind of union Cesar Chavez wanted.

Cesar Chavez poses beside a protest sign that reads Huelga, the Spanish word for strike.

To him, a union was more than a collection of laborers; it was a community—*una causa*. This kind of union would offer people proper respect and rewards for their hard work. Working to build such a community of farm-workers became Cesar Chavez's life goal. Some called him a labor leader, others a political activist. As for Cesar himself, he was simply happy and proud to be called the farmworker's friend.

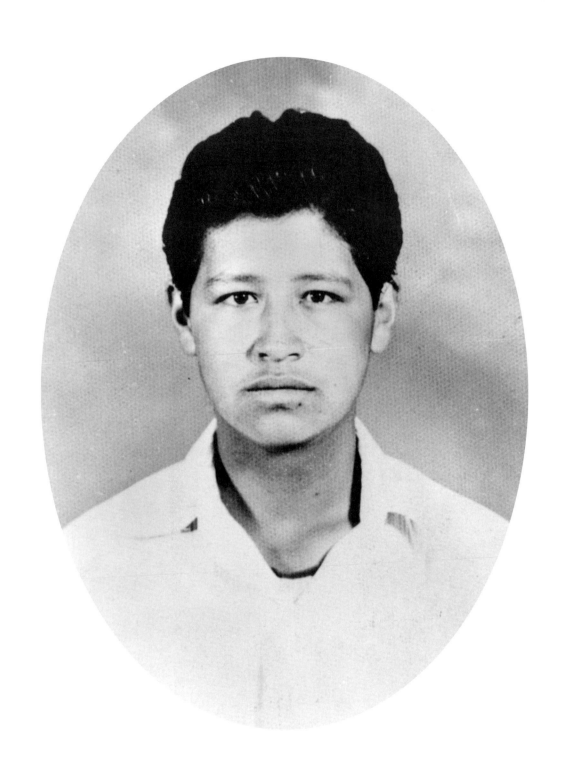

Chapter 1

IN THE FIELDS

Slowly eleven-year-old Cesar Chavez stood on his toes and stretched his body in the blazing California sunlight. His tired muscles ached. He wiped his sweat-covered face with the thin sleeve of his shirt. How long had he been picking peas in the field? Three hours seemed like ten on hot days like this one. The minutes dragged along slowly, almost as slowly as the peas piled up in the bottom of Cesar's basket.

The boy glanced over at his father and mother, both bent at the waist, plucking peas and putting them in their own baskets. Nearby, his brothers and sisters did the same. Once the baskets were full, other workers sorted the peas, tossing aside those not suitable for sale. The pea pickers got credit only for the good peas. In three hours of work, the entire Chavez family earned only twenty cents.

Left: Cesar and his sister Rita in Arizona. *Below:* Cesar was only nine months old when this photograph was taken.

   Young Cesar Chavez did not think about money while he picked peas with the other migrant workers. Instead, he liked to remember the times before his family worked in the fields.

   Cesar Estrada Chavez was born on March 31, 1927, above the family store near Yuma, Arizona. Growing up in Arizona, Cesar had often played in his father's pool hall. Once he was old enough, Cesar helped sell candy behind the store counter.

   His father, Librado Chavez, not only ran a pool hall and a small store, he also helped on his own parents' 160-acre farm. Often Cesar's father worked sixteen hours a day, from sunup to sundown. But he was never too tired to make toys for his children or to take them to the outdoor bathroom at night. In the Arizona moonlight, Librado Chavez would carry a daughter or small son to the outhouse some distance away. No desert coyote or wolf ever dared to challenge the strong, sturdy figure.

While Librado worked, Juana Chavez, Cesar's mother, kept close watch over the family. A petite woman with long black hair, Juana Chavez was known for her big heart. To Juana, being a good Roman Catholic meant more than merely going to Mass every week. It meant reaching out and helping people every day. Sometimes she sent Cesar and his younger brother Richard out to look for hungry tramps. "We always have enough for one more of God's children," said Juana.

Unable to read or write, Cesar's mother was a gifted storyteller. Her proverbs, or *dichos,* as they were called in Spanish, were short tales neatly summed up in a brief moral or lesson for living. "What you do to others, others do to you," she would say. "If you're in the honey," Juana told her children, "some of it will stick to you." Each piece of advice, or *consejo,* demanded careful thought. "He who never listens to consejos will never grow to be old," Cesar's mother warned.

Of all his mother's consejos, Cesar best remembered her advice about getting along with others. She had no use for fighting, despite the fact that Hispanic culture promoted the idea of a man defending himself. Juana Chavez admonished her children when challenged to "use your mind and mouth to talk things out." She'd say, "It takes two to fight."

Juana Chavez greatly influenced her son Cesar.

Usually, Cesar took his mother's advice. However, now and then his temper took over. Once, when an older cousin grabbed the family cat and twirled it around, Cesar exploded in anger. He ran into the house and seized his father's old shotgun. Cesar knew the weapon wasn't loaded, but his cousin didn't. Cesar's cousin dropped the cat and took off running.

Cesar had been surrounded by cousins, aunts, and uncles when he was growing up in the North Gila River Valley near Yuma. Librado and Juana Chavez came from big families. As a boy, Cesar counted some 180 cousins living on farms and in surrounding villages.

Cesar's world changed forever by his tenth birthday. In the 1930s, the Great Depression struck the United States. Businesses and banks failed across the nation, and people lost their jobs.

When Cesar was young, the Chavez family lived in the North Gila River Valley near Yuma, Arizona.

At the same time, a severe drought dried up streams in the southwestern United States. The Gila River, once full and flowing, turned into a dry, snaky outline. Fertile fields became clay crusts. Corn and squash crops on the Chavez family farm withered away, and few customers came into the pool hall and store. No one in the area had money to spend. Without crops and customers, the Chavez family struggled to pay its bills.

In 1937 the struggle ended. The state of Arizona demanded money owed on taxes, and when Librado Chavez could not pay, he was ordered out of his home and off his land. He headed to California, joining thousands of other Americans who had lost their farms. As soon as he could, Librado sent for his wife and children.

As migrant workers, the Chavezes lived in small run-down shacks or tents in crowded camps. Often there was no plumbing or electricity. There were no places for children to play. Cesar and his brothers and sisters attended school for a few weeks at a time, until a crop was harvested. Then the family moved on. Cesar waged a constant battle to keep up with his lessons. At home, everyone spoke Spanish. But in school, teachers insisted their students speak English. Often Cesar put his head down on his desk and fell asleep.

While some of his friends fished in the California canals for fun, Cesar fished to help feed his family. He picked wild mustard greens too, regularly carrying home full baskets. He and his brother Richard collected tinfoil from empty cigarette packages to earn spending money.

Migrant workers harvest carrots in the 1930s. Young Cesar Chavez worked in fields like these, harvesting crops, but he never got used to migrant life.

They rolled the shiny paper into a giant ball. The ball weighed eighteen pounds when they took it to a Mexican junk dealer. With the money they received, the two boys treated themselves to a pair of tennis shoes and two sweatshirts.

Librado and Juana appreciated their sons' efforts. Earning a living back in Yuma had never been easy, but a migrant farmworker's life was much more difficult. Every penny helped the family survive. Every day meant a new search for work.

Whenever Librado Chavez heard about another crop to be harvested, he packed up his family. They drove to the farm that needed workers. Sometimes they arrived too late. All the workers were hired. Sometimes there were so many migrants needing work that the grower reduced the wages he had first offered. More than once the entire Chavez family worked for a whole day and earned only a dollar or two.

From the beginning, Cesar hated being a migrant worker. Maybe he hated it because he had known a different way of life. Back in Arizona, he knew his family was poor, always struggling to pay bills, but at least the Chavezes were free. To Cesar, migrants were poor and chained to their way of life. The only thing that changed was the crop to be harvested.

Juana Chavez worked to keep the family's spirits up. No one was allowed to complain. "There's always someone worse off than us," she told her family. At times that was hard for Cesar to believe. Cesar wore his shoes until they fell apart. Then he walked barefoot, squishing his feet in the mud. If there was not enough room for all of his family in the migrant worker villages, Cesar sometimes slept under bridges nearby.

Eventually the family found a more permanent home. Around San Jose, California, south of San Francisco, there were many fields and orchards. Area landowners often hired migrant workers. Librado found a small house in a Spanish-speaking neighborhood, or *barrio,* in the city and moved his family there. The area was called *Sal Si Puedes,* or Get Out If You Can. Cesar soon discovered what that meant. Few people ever earned enough money to get out of Sal Si Puedes. The neighborhood was crowded with families living elbow to elbow. For Cesar, there was no privacy, no time to be alone.

Many migrant workers grew tired of poor living conditions, long hours, and low pay. Librado Chavez, his brother, and other farmworkers joined labor unions. By joining together in a union, field-workers could bargain with farm owners as a group, not one by one. Union members hoped that growers might pay more attention to their demands when those demands came from a large group of workers.

Sometimes union members came to the Chavez house to meet. Cesar listened to people talk about their jobs and lives. Discussions became shouting matches, as tired workers shared their anger and frustration. Finally, Librado and other union members demanded changes from the growers. When the growers would not listen, union members left their jobs. *"Huelga!"* they shouted, the Spanish word for strike.

Housing for migrant workers near Fresno, California, in the 1930s

The growers stood firm. Day and night the workers marched, carrying posters and shouting their demands. But their money and patience ran out. They gave up their strike and went back to work.

Cesar wondered if workers ever *could* win a strike. All that time spent marching and shouting for change didn't amount to much when everyone went back to work with nothing to show for it. Cesar knew the workers were determined to get more respect, but he also knew how hard it was to go to bed at night hungry. An empty stomach, Cesar realized, made it hard to fight, even when you knew you were right.

Cesar Chavez received a diploma after graduating from the eighth grade, but his father's accident kept him from finishing his high school education.

Chapter 2

TROUBLED TIMES

In 1942 tragedy struck the Chavez family when Librado Chavez was injured in a car accident. During his long recovery, he was unable to work. Cesar made a big decision. The fifteen-year-old boy left school. Once things were better at home, Cesar planned to return to complete his education. Juana Chavez was not happy with the decision, yet she understood. No money came into the family coffers when a child was attending school. A day's work in the fields could bring in fifty or sixty cents.

In the fields and at home, Cesar took on more and more responsibility. In the past, Librado Chavez had decided when and where the family would move to harvest a crop. But gradually the older man saw that Cesar understood when it was time to trim the lettuce and which growers paid the best wages. The calendar for the Chavez family revolved around crops, and Cesar knew the state of California by its fruit and vegetable harvests.

At sixteen Cesar took over driving the family car. His brother Richard handled the mechanical end of the 1930 Studebaker, setting the spark plugs and keeping the engine lubed and oiled. Even after their father recovered some of his strength and returned to the fields, the brothers kept their new duties.

For a few years, Cesar followed the yearly round of melon picking, broccoli harvesting, cherry picking, and beet topping. Finally in 1944, the seventeen-year-old boy could take no more. While thinning out a row of sugar beets one day, Cesar suddenly stood up and said, "Dad, I've had it!"

Cesar marched off and didn't stop marching until he reached the local recruiting office. He joined the United States Navy. The nation was at war, and Cesar hoped that life in the navy would offer him new opportunities. He soon discovered that most Hispanic sailors served as deckhands—nothing more and nothing less.

Before Cesar *(far right)* joined the navy, he and Richard *(far left)* hung out with friends in Sal Si Puedes.

At age 17, Cesar joined the United States Navy.

While World War II raged, Cesar went from boat to boat, sometimes working at sea and other times docked in a harbor. He never faced combat action, coming only as close as the Mariana Islands, where the guns and shelling remained far away.

Cesar welcomed any break from his navy service and was glad to return home on leave. During one visit to the Chavez family in Delano, California, Cesar and a couple of navy buddies went off to a movie. All the movie theaters around Delano were segregated. No law said that whites should sit in one section, and everyone else in the back or balcony. But it was understood. On this particular night, Cesar didn't feel like sitting in a segregated section. He was out of uniform, and he just wanted to have a good time. Despite an usherette's warning, he plopped down in a seat that was off-limits to Hispanics.

Minutes later, the assistant manager of the movie house asked Cesar to move. He refused to budge. Finally, the police were called. The officers pried Cesar's hands loose from the armrests and carted him off to jail.

During World War II, Cesar *(far left)* made friends in the navy, but he didn't see combat duty.

For the next hour, Cesar sat impatiently while the desk sergeant at the police station tried to figure out how to charge the young sailor. Cesar wasn't drunk or disorderly. He wasn't disturbing the peace. He hadn't broken any written law. According to Cesar, "It was just a question that I wanted a free choice of where I wanted to be."

When Cesar was finally released, he was angry—angry because of what had happened and even more angry because he knew he should have done more to fight against this unfair treatment. If he'd only known what to say and what to do in such a situation. But this was the first time he'd stood up for his rights. Somehow, he knew there would be other incidents like this one in the future. Then, he promised himself, he *would* know what to do.

Chapter 3

SEEKING DIRECTION

In 1945 World War II ended, and soon Cesar's stint in the service was over. Cesar rejoined his parents, sisters, and brothers living in Delano. Juana Chavez welcomed her nineteen-year-old son home by preparing his favorite dish—spicy hot burritos. Cesar could not get enough. No more of that awful navy food. How he hated it! It was good to be back. Cesar's smile and laugh came easily now, and he sported a light mustache to look older.

Soon after his return, Cesar began spending more time with Helen Fabela. The two had dated for several years, and Cesar enjoyed being with the dark-haired beauty with flowers in her hair. She, too, came from a big family. Although her parents weren't migrant workers, they did work in the fields, cutting cotton for a Delano farmer. Cesar and Helen dated inexpensively—a walk in the moonlight or perhaps a movie—since Cesar had returned to migrant work and did not have much spending money. The couple liked being together, whatever they did.

Cesar and Helen in 1948

Once more Cesar lived his life by the harvest calendar. In the summer, he headed to the vineyards to pick grapes. During the winter, he picked cotton in the fields. Now and then, he stashed away a little money for a special occasion.

That occasion arrived in 1948 when Cesar asked Helen to marry him. She agreed. They were wed in a civil ceremony in Reno, Nevada, on October 22, 1948. Then the couple returned to San Jose, California, for a church wedding. After a two-week honeymoon trip, Cesar and Helen settled into a new life.

For the next few years, Cesar took whatever work he could find, harvesting grapes in the vineyards outside Delano, picking apricots near San Jose, and raising strawberries. The work was always hard and the pay was disappointing. All the same, Cesar and Helen found much to celebrate. The arrival of a son, Fernando, lifted the couple's spirits yet added to their financial burdens. Soon, the couple had another baby, this time a girl named Sylvia. And Helen was pregnant again.

Tired of migrant work, Cesar walked the streets of San Jose, visiting any store or business that might need an able worker. The jobs were filled. Then he heard that a lumber factory in Crescent City was hiring. Where was Crescent City? Cesar didn't know. Still, he *did* know that anything was better than working in the fields.

Cesar, Richard, and three of their cousins jumped in a car and headed north. Crescent City was four hundred miles away, and none of the car's occupants had ever been there. All of them were willing to take a chance on being hired.

Juana and Librado Chavez lived in Delano, California, in the 1940s.

The chance paid off. For the first time in his life, Cesar began earning money away from the fields. The lumber work was harder than any planting and picking Cesar had ever done. At the end of each day, all he could do was collapse on a cot and sleep until the next morning.

But as Cesar and Richard got used to the work, their jobs became easier. The weekly paychecks were also a welcome sight. Richard, always the handyman, started building a small house so they could bring their families up from San Jose. Soon after Helen's arrival in Crescent City, a daughter Linda was born.

With a steady paycheck coming in and with his wife and three young children surrounding him, Cesar felt satisfied with his life. If only it didn't rain so much in northern California. Almost every day brought a downpour, and the winds howled all winter. For a year and a half, Cesar and his family tolerated the bad weather.

When word reached Crescent City that lumber workers were needed back in San Jose, no coaxing was needed. Cesar and Richard both gathered up their families and headed south. Once back in San Jose, Richard struck out on his own as a carpenter. Cesar hired on at a local lumber mill.

At about this time, Cesar met Father Donald McDonnell. The Catholic priest said Mass for the migrant workers around San Jose. Cesar helped Father McDonnell fix up an old hall where Masses could be held. Side by side, the two men hammered together old benches and repainted them. The work sessions offered a chance to visit and share ideas.

Both men were about the same age, and both knew much about migrants. Cesar had spent most of his adult life working in the fields, while the priest had studied and learned through books and articles. The priest shared all he had read and learned. "I knew a lot about the work, but I didn't know anything about the economics," Cesar remembered later, "and I learned quite a bit from him."

Father McDonnell was always willing to loan books to Cesar too. The reading was not always easy for Cesar, but the priest was there to answer questions. Special Senate hearings about agriculture had been held in 1940. Cesar read transcripts of those meetings and talked to Father McDonnell about them. He quickly discovered that farming was much more than planting and harvesting. There were complicated rules about bank loans for land investments, for equipment and implement purchases, and for seed buying.

But Cesar read about more than just agriculture. He also read about people who had helped to change things and to fight injustice. He enjoyed reading about the gentle and humble Saint Francis of Assisi. In the 1200s, Francis, an Italian Catholic, devoted his life to feeding and helping the poor. Cesar liked reading about the determined statesman Mohandas Gandhi too. A Hindu lawyer from India, Gandhi had used nonviolent action to secure independence from Great Britain for the Indian people. Cesar realized that Francis of Assisi and Mohandas Gandhi were much like his own mother, always reaching out to help the poor and always trying to keep the peace among people.

Like Saint Francis of Assisi, Mohandas Gandhi, and Juana Chavez, Cesar, too, wanted to help people. Anyone around him sensed it immediately. When people spoke to him, he listened to every word they said. He passed along what he had read and what Father McDonnell had told him. Wherever Cesar went, he attracted a crowd.

In June of 1952, a man named Fred Ross came to Sal Si Puedes looking for Cesar Chavez. Ross was an organizer for the Community Services Organization, or CSO. Ross's job was to help organize people living in California's Mexican-American barrios. When Ross asked around for someone to help him, everyone told him to talk to Cesar Chavez.

Fred Ross, shown here in 1975, was an organizer for the Community Services Organization, or CSO.

But Chavez did not want to talk with Ross. Others like Ross had come to the barrio, claiming they wanted to help Mexican-American families. The visitors always asked lots of questions and then disappeared. Nothing good ever came of those visits. Why would this one be different?

Chavez hid from Ross, slipping across the street to his brother's house whenever the community organizer knocked on his door. But Ross kept coming back. Finally, Helen grew tired of the hide-and-seek game. She pointed out Richard's house, and Ross caught up with Cesar Chavez.

Once the two men sat down to talk, Chavez changed his attitude a bit. Ross *did* seem different from others who had come to the barrio. He seemed honest and sincere in wanting to help Mexican Americans. By the time their meeting ended, Chavez had offered his home as a place for Ross to talk with families from the barrio. All the same, Chavez wasn't sure he trusted Ross. Later, he talked to a few of his friends and made a plan. If Ross said anything out of line, Chavez would move his cigarette from his right hand to his left. That was a signal to create trouble and toss Ross out.

Chavez never gave that signal. From the moment Fred Ross started speaking at the meeting, he showed sensitivity and understanding for barrio residents and their lives. He talked about the big packing house that was dumping waste into a creek behind Sal Si Puedes. Many children played in the creek and developed sores. Huge swarms of mosquitoes hovered in the area. Ross said the politicians should get the bugs out. He also said that the CSO was trying to do just that. He discussed other CSO programs and suggested how Mexican Americans could help themselves.

Chavez walked Ross out to his car after the meeting. Chavez had many questions. How could he go about organizing people in his neighborhood to gain power? What should he do next? he asked.

CSO staff members and volunteers worked throughout California to register Mexican Americans to vote.

"I have another meeting now," Ross answered. "I don't suppose you'd like to come?"

"Oh, yes, I would!" Chavez replied instantly. He was eager to soak in more of Ross's ideas, and he wanted to study the way Ross presented them. According to Ross, even poor people could have power over their lives.

"We had never thought that we could actually have any say in our lives," Chavez recalled. "We were poor, we knew it, and we were beyond helping ourselves. Fred Ross opened our eyes—and our minds—to what power we *could* have."

That night, June 9, 1952, marked a turning point in Cesar Chavez's life. He wanted to do what Fred Ross was doing. But it would not be easy. Cesar knew he lacked formal education and experience. Yet he did know the people. He was one of them. He understood their thinking, their hopes and dreams. Surely that counted for something. Maybe the rest could be learned. Just the thought of helping his people gave Cesar Chavez new hope for the future.

Chapter 4

ANOTHER KIND OF HARVEST

Cesar gazed down at the papers on the table before him. Some sheets contained names, while others were maps and graphs. It was like a giant game. Fred Ross explained what was on each paper. Facts and statistics, numbers and laws—Cesar listened to everything. It became clear to him that many Mexican Americans were not voting. Cesar and Fred believed that people did not realize how important their votes were.

"The ballot is a citizen's certificate of raw power," Fred said often. With those words echoing in his mind, Cesar walked door-to-door in San Jose. No matter how tired he was after working at the lumberyard during the day, Cesar spent his evenings calling on Mexican Americans who were not registered to vote. In a way, it was like working in the fields again, but this time he was planting the seeds for hope and action.

While working for the CSO, Cesar Chavez, second from the right, helped organize Mexican Americans living in barrios.

For the next eighty-five nights leading up to the registration deadline, Cesar patiently explained the benefits of voting. Only registered voters, he said, could put people in office who would help Mexican Americans and take care of their needs.

Cesar and the CSO helped to sign up six thousand new voters. In November of 1952, many of these Mexican Americans went to the polls for the first time. But troubles arose quickly. Some election officials challenged the first-time voters. The officials questioned whether the Mexican Americans could read or write. Confused and angry, many people left the polls without voting.

Cesar had worked hard registering voters. Now he realized that his work did not end with the election. Fred told Cesar that they could protest the actions of the election officials by sending written complaints to the attorney general of California. Some of the CSO board members, who had government jobs, refused to sign any written protest for fear of some kind of reprisal. Disgusted with those who would not stand up for what was right, Cesar did not hesitate. "I'll sign the protest," he volunteered.

Complaints against election officials grabbed major headlines in the newspapers. Those accused responded, charging the CSO with registering illegal immigrants and dead people. It turned into a battle of name-calling, and Cesar's own name appeared in print.

One day Cesar's boss at the lumberyard came running. "The FBI wants to see you!" he said. Within minutes two FBI agents started asking Cesar questions about communism. It all stemmed from the CSO complaint against election officials. Some people in power believed that anyone who challenged the government was a communist.

"You know damn well I'm not a Communist!" Cesar shot back.

Despite his denials, Cesar Chavez was labeled a communist by the local newspaper. In the weeks and months that followed, others asked Cesar if he was a communist.

"No," came the answer.

"How do we know?"

Cesar shook his head. "You don't know. You know because I tell you."

Cesar's friends and coworkers wanted to believe him. How could they mistrust a man who always took other people's problems as his own, trying to find solutions for their difficulties?

Many of Cesar's neighbors could not read or write English well, some not at all. Cesar showed them how to apply for United States citizenship and how to interpret government papers. Some of the people were easy targets for crooked salesmen. Cesar listened and told them how to report their losses. Whatever the problem, Cesar offered to help. If he didn't know the answer, he went to Fred Ross. When Fred hit a snag, his CSO boss back in Chicago, Saul Alinsky, could usually supply the answers. Cesar went back to people and told them what he had learned. The word spread: "If you have trouble, . . . Chavez can help."

More and more people returned to seek Cesar's guidance. He gave his time and advice freely. Then, when *he* needed volunteers to help with CSO meetings, he called upon those he had helped. These meetings, held in the volunteer's house, gave the organization a family atmosphere. People shared their problems and listened to each other. They planned social get-togethers, such as dinners and dances too.

With Fred's training and advice, Cesar helped the groups elect their own officers and stand on their own feet. The process—from house meetings to the election of officers—usually took about three months. Then Cesar would move on to another neighborhood to help start another group.

Saul Alinsky, head of the Industrial Areas Foundation, founded the CSO.

Fred Ross's boss, Saul Alinsky, liked what Cesar Chavez was doing around San Jose. When the lumberyard started laying off employees, Cesar found himself out of a job. That didn't last long. Alinsky and Ross knew Chavez was ready to handle full-time work with the CSO in San Jose. With an ever-growing family, Cesar couldn't refuse the job offer. Soon he faced even more responsibility.

Cesar Chavez had shown he could get people organized in small towns and neighborhoods in and around San Jose. Now, Fred Ross and Saul Alinsky wondered if he could do the same thing in a big city. Could he do it alone, without Ross nearby? What about a place like Oakland, California? It was an area ready for CSO activities. Could Cesar Chavez plant the seeds for organizing people there? Alinsky and Ross decided to give Chavez the chance. His salary would be thirty-five dollars a week. It was more money than Cesar had ever earned.

Now it was Cesar's turn to wonder if he was ready. He talked the opportunity over with Helen. As usual, she stood behind him. So did his parents and his brothers and sisters. Their support helped Cesar decide. With more than a little hesitation, he accepted the position.

Father Gerald Cox, a local priest, helped Chavez set up the first house meeting in Oakland. On the night of the meeting, Cesar had to force himself to go inside. Most of the people present were middle-aged women. Twenty-five-year-old Cesar, five feet six inches tall and skinny, cowered in a dark corner. He watched and listened.

"Well, it's getting late," one woman finally said. "I wonder where the organizer is."

"Well, I'm the organizer," Cesar blurted out.

The people looked at him with skepticism. Who was this kid sent to meet with them? What could he know?

Cesar tried to offer answers. He explained how the CSO worked and what it could do to help them. He searched for the right words to say, convinced that no one was paying much attention. In his mind, the meeting was a disaster. Yet before the people left, they were talking about having more meetings. Whether they felt sorry for Cesar, or honestly felt the evening was useful, they wanted to meet again. Another seed was planted.

The CSO came to Oxnard, California, in the late 1950s. When Cesar Chavez took over local organizing efforts, he relied on the help of many volunteers.

Chapter 5

SHOWDOWN AT OXNARD

In the weeks that followed, Cesar threw himself into organizing one meeting after another. Each night, after everyone was gone, he analyzed what was said. Why did people fall silent when they did—or argue? How could *he* have been more effective? Cesar seldom felt satisfied with his own performance.

After three months of individual house meetings in Oakland, Cesar planned a big group gathering at Saint Mary's Church. He told everyone to spread the word. A good turnout meant there was real interest in getting things done, of gaining some political power for Mexican Americans in the area. Would anybody come? Nervously, Cesar hoped and prayed.

Only twenty people had arrived at the church by the time the meeting was scheduled to begin. Another disaster, Cesar thought. But as the minutes ticked away, people streamed in. By evening's end, over three hundred people filled the hall. Cesar's worried frown became a wide smile.

Fred Ross smiled too, when he heard the news. Until that night, Fred had always set up and planned big meetings. Now Cesar had shown that he could do that on his own. It was a big step.

An even bigger step followed. Delighted with reports of the meeting at Saint Mary's, Fred laid out a new target area for Cesar. It was time to plant some CSO seeds in Madera and the surrounding San Joaquin Valley. The territory was bigger, and so was the salary. From thirty-five dollars a week, it jumped to fifty-eight.

The raise in pay came in handy. Cesar and Helen now had four mouths to feed besides their own. Fernando, Sylvia, Linda, and Eloise all joined their parents in moving to Madera. Cesar wished for more time with his family, but his job kept him away from home a lot.

From Madera, Cesar took his family to Bakersfield, and then on to Hanford. At each stop, the forceful and energetic organizer planted seeds for the CSO, starting house meetings, citizenship classes, and voter registration drives. Then, in a few months, he moved on to another town. When it was a choice of moving his family or traveling alone, Cesar went alone. He missed his family when they were not with him, yet he hated to have them always packing and leaving a place. That was too much like being a migrant family, and Cesar Chavez had put that part of his life behind him. Now, he wanted to do all he could to help those who *had* to live that way.

In 1958 Cesar headed to Oxnard, California, a town about thirty-five miles from Los Angeles. As a boy, Cesar had spent the winter there, the worst winter of his life. The weather was foggy and wet, and the working conditions were terrible. A young school friend had been killed at a railroad crossing there. Oxnard held few good memories. Now Cesar was back to help register voters.

However, once he got to Oxnard and started registering people, Cesar discovered a bigger problem. Local growers avoided hiring Mexican Americans who lived in the area. Instead, the owners brought in *braceros,* migrant workers from Mexico. Braceros would work longer hours at lower wages. Federal laws stated that braceros should be used only if there were no local workers available. Clearly the growers were breaking the law.

To be sure of the situation, Cesar applied as a worker himself. First he went to a labor camp where he knew braceros worked. There he was told to go back into town to the office of the Farm Placement Service, or FPS. By the time he got to the office and filled out the forms, hours had passed. Once eligible to work, Cesar found all the jobs were taken by trucked-in braceros. Braceros didn't have to go to offices or fill out forms.

"Try tomorrow," Cesar was told, just as other area residents had been instructed. No way, Cesar decided. Instead, he organized a rally of Mexican Americans living in and around Oxnard.

Braceros, field hands from Mexico, were willing to work long hours for low pay.

On January 15, 1959, some fifteen hundred people gathered to hear Cesar speak. His volunteers distributed leaflets around the city, protesting the actions of the farm owners. Cesar called the governor's office and California's department of employment. He persuaded other area Mexican Americans to apply for work as he did. When they were refused too, he had more documentation of unfair hiring.

When Cesar and other CSO officials sat down with leaders of the Farm Placement Service, the FPS agreed to hire three local workers. Soon the three were let go, one for "lack of experience." The fellow had worked in the fields for seventeen years.

Cesar continued to fight. He led Mexican Americans in picketing the FPS office and the labor camps where braceros stayed overnight. The protesters carried placards and shouted, "We Want Jobs!" and "We Deserve to Work!"

To create even more publicity, Cesar then called every newspaper reporter and TV person in the area. He urged them to be at an employment office in Oxnard the next morning. They were there when Cesar led some seventy of his volunteers in filling out work applications. No one expected to be hired, and no one was.

From the employment office, Cesar led his group—and the reporters—to a nearby ranch. A man named Jones owned the sprawling ranch and hired braceros every day. When Cesar's marchers approached the Jones ranch, many asked what they should do next. At the gate, one fellow leaped on top of a car, urging the marchers to trespass. "We have to show these guys!" the man yelled.

Cesar jumped on top of another car. He wanted no part of a violent demonstration. "I'm not going," he said firmly. "If you go, I'm not responsible for what happens."

The people stood behind Cesar. Sensing the people's support, Cesar declared that they should never have to register to work again. What did it matter if they registered? They didn't get jobs anyway. With the media recording every moment, Cesar urged the workers to burn their registration forms, making a handsome bonfire. Satisfied that they had done all they could, Cesar dispersed the crowd.

In the weeks that followed, nothing seemed to happen. When he learned that United States Secretary of Labor James Mitchell was going to speak in nearby Ventura, Cesar quickly organized a march. One thousand Mexican Americans greeted Mitchell when his plane landed at the airport. They followed Mitchell into town, shouting, "We want jobs!" By nightfall, the candle-carrying marchers moved into Oxnard, singing Mexican hymns. When the police threatened to arrest Cesar for leading an illegal parade, he would not step aside. If the police arrested Cesar Chavez, his followers insisted they be arrested too.

What could the police do? Their jail would never hold all the protesters. Cesar and his followers marched forward with a police escort.

Slowly and reluctantly, area growers gave in. They even agreed to hire people right out of the CSO office. The FPS made changes too, removing some top officers from their jobs.

Encouraged by his successes at Oxnard, Cesar asked the CSO to establish a union for farmworkers. The people who worked the soil needed better working conditions, Cesar felt. They were entitled to fair pay and benefits. Despite his constant pleas for a union, Cesar's voice was ignored. Saul Alinsky and other CSO officials felt that the CSO could provide farmworkers with the tools to help themselves. To Alinsky and others, a union was unnecessary.

Cesar had learned a great deal in Oxnard. For the first time, he had felt capable of organizing and leading. Listening to the people and their needs; documenting abuses; organizing picket lines and marches; getting media publicity; and knowing how far to go and how firm to stand were all important to reaching goals. A union of farmworkers could achieve its own goals by doing the same things. Cesar remained convinced of that. If only he could convince others of the need. Someday, he thought, it could happen.

Dolores Huerta, a CSO organizer, agreed with Cesar Chavez on the need to form a union for farmworkers.

Chapter 6

"VIVA LA CAUSA!"

The leaders of the CSO knew Cesar was unhappy with them, and they did not want to lose his valuable talents. To make sure he stayed with the CSO, they offered him a position as national director in Los Angeles and a pay increase to $150 a week.

Cesar accepted the offer. After all, there were eight young Chavezes—Fernando, Sylvia, Linda, Eloise, Liz, Paul, Anna, and Anthony—to feed and clothe. Helen had sacrificed a great deal so that Cesar could travel and work with his people. She was always at home to care for the children, whenever they had problems or needs. Cesar wanted to offer his wife and family all that he could.

From 1959 until 1962, Cesar continued to work for the CSO. But some of the energy and enthusiasm left him. When he visited Oxnard six months after winning the battle for worker rights, everything had returned to the way it was before. The braceros were back working in the fields and the farm owners did as they pleased.

Cesar became convinced that there would be no lasting changes for the farmworkers unless they were organized. After many sleepless nights, he made a major decision. With Helen's support and $1,200 in the bank, Cesar resigned from the CSO. How did he feel about taking such a step? "Frightened, very frightened," Cesar remembered, but he knew it was something he *had* to do.

Cesar packed up his family and returned to Delano. There, if times got too bad, Helen's family could help out. Cesar laid out a map of all the towns and farmworkers' camps in the area. There were eighty-six, and Cesar promised to visit every one of them. His goal was to encourage workers to form a new union. It would be called the National Farm Workers Association, or NFWA.

Others had tried to organize farmworkers in the past, but they had been only partially successful. The Agricultural Workers Organizing Committee, or AWOC, had been formed in 1959, but few Mexican Americans had joined that union. It operated under the wing of the AFL-CIO, a huge national labor federation. Cesar wanted his people to run their own organization and reach for their own goals. At the age of thirty-five, Cesar vowed to form an independent union.

Setting up an office in his garage, Cesar ran off literature about the NFWA on an old mimeograph machine loaned to him by a minister, Reverend Jim Drake. Then he took the old but trusty family station wagon on the road. Wherever he could find an interested farm laborer or two, he would stop and chat about the new farmworkers' union.

Once Cesar Chavez started building the farmworkers' union, he turned to Reverend Wayne C. Hartmire, at right, and others for help.

Cesar's energy and interest won him valuable assistants. Dolores Huerta, one of the CSO's top workers, joined Chavez. So did Reverend Wayne C. Hartmire, a clergyman who knew how to get Protestants involved in the farmworkers' movement. (Cesar's efforts had attracted mostly Catholic migrants.) Cesar's cousin Manuel gave up a steady job selling cars in San Diego, to aid the effort.

Not everyone was so easily persuaded. Earlier efforts to gain rights for farmworkers had failed. Government officials and growers had been able to block anyone trying to bring the migrants together as an organized group.

The flag Manuel Chavez designed for the National Farm Workers
Association, or NFWA, caused controversy but was given full support
by the union's leader, Cesar Chavez.

Even the National Labor Relations Act, which protected most laborers, didn't provide for farmworkers. Some people wondered how Chavez could make a difference.

But the short, small-framed man focused on every word people said, and his eyes sparkled with interest and concern. Cesar never promised quick solutions; he simply offered to help if he could. When people learned he had given up a paid job to try to organize farmworkers, they were even more impressed.

On September 30, 1962, Cesar Chavez took a major step. He called together all interested farmworkers for a meeting in an abandoned theater in Fresno, California. Over two hundred people attended the first official convention of the NFWA. Cesar presided, sharing his goals and dreams. Working together, Cesar said, farmworkers could meet those goals.

Dolores Huerta spoke too, backing up Cesar's ideas and plans. Manuel Chavez revealed a special surprise— a flag for the union. The scarlet flag with a stylized black eagle on a white circle quickly caused controversy. To some, it looked like a nazi symbol. To Cesar and to others, it represented an organized group of people seeking fair treatment. It was, he said, "a strong beautiful sign of hope."

Cesar did not want people viewing his union as just another labor group. He wanted the NFWA to be a community, *una causa*. It might have a constitution, officers, dues, and other labor union ingredients, but the NFWA would also be a family, an organization that represented the needs of its members. As the delegates settled down and elected leaders, they put together a framework for their group. *Viva la causa!* or "Long live the cause!" was picked by the members as their motto. When dues of $3.50 a month were decided upon, many members wondered where they would find the money. But by sacrificing for the cause, they would feel they were investing in something worthwhile and building for the future— *their* future.

The convention in Fresno was a great success, yet within months, many of those who had signed up at the beginning dropped by the wayside. Paying members dropped from two hundred to twelve. Sometimes Cesar wondered if the union would survive. Many people came, asked questions, got answers, and then dropped out. No one seemed to want to help anyone but himself. At times, Cesar felt alone in trying to hold the union together. He promised to give the cause three full years. If it wasn't a united group by then, he would give up.

Cesar worked all the harder, driving to this house and that, speaking, listening, and collecting dues. The work was tiring, but slowly and steadily the NFWA membership grew. Cesar looked around for a chance to capture the public spotlight and attract the attention of even more people. That opportunity came in September 1965.

Among the most miserable spots for migrants to work were the vineyards around Delano. Under a scorching sun and in one hundred degree temperatures, grape pickers hunched over for hours, harvesting fruit. Bugs leaped from under every leaf, crawling onto sweating hands and arms. The wages were poor, often less than one dollar an hour. Vineyard workers sometimes found themselves doused with insect-killing chemical sprays. Toilets were few and far between. If clean drinking water was provided, workers often had to rent a cup to quench their thirst.

Despite the difficult conditions, workers in the vineyards enjoyed a major advantage over most migrants. Grape cultivation stretched over ten months, allowing workers an extended time in one place. Vineyard workers were luckier than most, but in September of 1965, after a drastic pay cut, they were ready to rebel. The mostly Filipino members of the AWOC called a strike for September 8.

Larry Itliong, AWOC's leader, went to Cesar Chavez. Surely Chavez could recognize the poor wages and treatment of the grape pickers. Would Chavez and the NFWA join Itliong and the AWOC in this strike?

Cesar left the decision up to NFWA members. He presented the reasons for the strike at a meeting on September 16, Mexican Independence Day. The vote was unanimous; the NFWA would help AWOC workers in their fight against the growers.

There was little chance that the grape pickers' strike would be swiftly resolved. The vineyard owners were wealthy and could hold out for a long time. Although the workers were poor, they were willing to do whatever it took—and for as long as it took—to get the changes that they wanted.

Cesar realized it was important to involve more than just the NFWA, the AWOC, and the growers in this strike.

When vineyard workers went on strike, their leader, Larry Itliong *(front row, far right),* asked Cesar Chavez and the NFWA to join the workers in their struggle.

If the general public knew about the situation, they might pressure the growers to bargain with the workers. If people knew and understood the problems of the vineyard workers, Cesar was convinced the strike could be won.

In the weeks that followed, Cesar took his cause to anyone who would listen. Cesar not only talked about the strike against the vineyard owners, he also talked about the needs of all farmworkers. He spoke of a worker's right to be respected and about the low wages paid to farmworkers.

Wages *were* low. In 1965 the average yearly income of California farm laborers was $1,350—well below the poverty line of $3,100 set by the national government.

While Cesar worked to make people more aware of the farmworkers' financial struggles, he also pondered other ways to dramatize their needs. After studying the situation, Cesar decided that focusing on one grower in the strike would be wiser than going after all of them. Collectively, the growers were rich and powerful, but if one caved in, others might follow. With other strike leaders, Cesar selected Schenley Industries, Inc., in Delano as a target. Picketers concentrated on Schenley's 3,350 cultivated acres. The NFWA and the AWOC urged everyone to boycott Schenley products.

From his readings, Chavez remembered that nonviolent marches had worked well for Mohandas Gandhi in India. He also knew that civil rights leaders in the south were leading their supporters on marches, demanding that blacks receive equal opportunities. Would such marches help the farmworkers of California too? Cesar wondered.

The march, or pilgrimage, to Sacramento, was meant to draw public attention to the problems of striking grape pickers. Cesar Chavez led the way.

After careful consideration, Cesar decided that it was worth a try. He called upon NFWA members to stage peaceful marches on agricultural offices around the state.

Then, in March of 1966, he kicked off a 250-mile march, or pilgrimage, from Delano to the California state capitol in Sacramento. The purpose was to ask Governor Edmund G. "Pat" Brown to hear union demands and to help settle the strike. Sixty-seven people began the march. By the time the farmworkers reached Sacramento on Easter Sunday, a crowd of ten thousand was waiting.

They cheered the weary travelers, causing the exhausted Cesar Chavez to flash a broad triumphant smile.

The march had been a success, gaining publicity for the strikers, getting the attention of government officials, and putting pressure on vineyard owners. After talks with Schenley leaders, Cesar announced that the company had agreed to recognize the NFWA as a union. Under the new contract, workers at Schenley won a pay raise of thirty-five cents an hour. The company also promised to contribute regularly to the NFWA credit union. It was the first union contract for farmworkers in American history. Chavez's cheerful face appeared in newspapers and magazines around the country.

Grateful for the publicity, Cesar knew there was much more to do. Schenley was just the first step. Cesar mapped out plans to go after another major farm near Delano, the Sierra Vista acreage run by the DiGiorgio Corporation. He asked people to boycott DiGiorgio products and directed his NFWA followers to picket outside Sierra Vista.

While Chavez talked to DiGiorgio officials, another union took action. Cesar had shown that farmworkers could be organized and powerful. Now the Teamsters Union, representing people in transport, wanted to grab the farmworkers' dues and power. Teamsters' leaders hoped to lure NFWA and AWOC members away from their unions.

At the same time, the AFL-CIO encouraged the NFWA to join with AWOC. Chavez agreed, and the United Farm Workers Organizing Committee, or UFWOC, was born.

When farmworkers at DiGiorgio's were allowed to choose between the Teamsters and the newly formed union, the UFWOC won a resounding victory.

Although Cesar was happy with the progress of his union, changes came slowly. Some UFWOC supporters suggested violence for faster action. Cesar squelched that idea fast. Instead, he once again followed the example of Mohandas Gandhi. On February 15, 1968, Cesar Chavez stopped eating. This dramatic action captured headlines around the country. As Cesar's fasting continued, more and more people followed his weakening condition. Why would anyone do this? many wondered.

More donations flowed in to help the UFWOC, and pressure increased for the growers to give in. In Europe, dockworkers refused to unload California grapes from ships. Satisfied that he had shown people the value of nonviolent action, Cesar started eating again twenty-five days after his fast had begun.

By the spring of 1969, after four years of picketing, marching, and fasting, Cesar was tired. Yet he stood firm. Cesar asked people across the nation to buy only grapes boxed with the UFWOC black eagle emblem. Any other grapes should be boycotted. Thanks to the efforts of Cesar Chavez and his followers, the public backed the boycott. Vineyard owners complained that boycotting cost them twenty-five million dollars. One by one, the growers agreed to Chavez's demands. In July of 1970, five years after the strike had begun, it ended. Most grape growers agreed to three-year contracts offering better wages, health insurance, and general benefits.

Nearing the end of his fast in 1968, Cesar Chavez showed the strain of his ordeal.

When several of California's biggest grape growers, represented by John Giumarra *(right),* signed a contract with the United Farm Workers Organizing Committee, Cesar Chavez and others cheered.

It was a major victory for Cesar, yet there was little time for celebration. Within a month, he was headed into another confrontation, a strike of lettuce workers in the Salinas Valley of California.

Cesar knew the new strike would be a challenge, but he felt sure of himself. That confidence rose every time he saw the flying black eagle on a box of grapes. To Cesar Chavez, the UFWOC emblem not only represented the men and women who had picked those grapes. It also reflected new rights and respect for all farmworkers.

Chapter 7

TOWARD THE SUNSET

In the summer of 1970, fourteen large lettuce growers in the Salinas Valley signed "sweetheart" contracts with the Teamsters. The deals were sweet for the transportation union and the growers. But farmworkers had not been allowed to vote and would gain little under the new contracts.

Cesar Chavez arrived on the scene to organize UFWOC members to fight both the Teamsters and the growers. On August 8, 1970, Chavez called a strike against the Salinas division of the Purex Company. The tactic of singling out one grower had worked in Delano—why not try it again? Within two weeks, the lettuce grower shut down. But the Teamsters and the other growers stood firm.

Cesar and Helen took a moment to relax with two of their eight children and a young friend in the late 1960s. Such moments were rare, however, since Cesar was in charge of a busy campaign of strikes, pickets, and boycotts.

Soon Cesar took another major step. He called for a general strike of all lettuce workers in the Salinas Valley. Some seven thousand workers stayed home, and forty farms were left without pickers. With the public starting to take an interest, Cesar urged people to boycott the lettuce of Bud Antle, another grower who had signed up with the Teamsters. Antle fought back, going to court to stop Chavez's boycott. Cesar refused to change his strategy, even when he was threatened with jail.

On December 4, 1970, he stood in a Salinas court-room. Over two thousand supporters crowded into the area, overflowing onto the surrounding block. As always, according to Cesar's orders, they were silent and nonviolent. Even when he was sent to jail, the farm-workers stood quietly.

Inside the jail, Cesar set up a strict schedule. He planned his reading, eating, and sleeping, his periods for exercise and writing, and his time for visits and meditation. His supporters set up picket lines around the jail, singing hymns and shouting cheers.

While Cesar Chavez was in jail, he had many visitors, including Ethel Kennedy, widow of the late senator Robert F. Kennedy.

In the meantime, UFWOC lawyers took Cesar's case to the California Supreme Court. The higher court ordered Chavez released on Christmas Eve while judges reviewed the case. "Jails were made for men who fight for their rights," Cesar told his supporters. "My spirit was never in jail. They can jail us, but they can never jail the Cause." Four months later, the California Supreme Court ruled that the UFWOC boycott against the lettuce growers was legal. Cesar Chavez was cleared of any charges.

At about this time, the Teamsters seemed to self-destruct. Union leaders were found guilty of misusing funds and possessing weapons. Facing problems within their organization, the Teamsters looked inward. Their fight with the UFWOC was over.

But the lettuce growers held out. Cesar decided to call a nationwide boycott of lettuce. He vowed to continue the boycott until the growers recognized the union. Cesar felt progress was being made, yet everything always seemed to take so long. Once, when asked how long it would take to get the farmworkers organized, Cesar answered, "A lifetime."

Cesar Chavez was willing to put in whatever time it took. "There is no life apart from the union," he declared. Working eighteen hours a day, he bounced around the country, going wherever he was asked or needed.

Cesar was devoted to his cause, but some people questioned that devotion. Critics claimed he wanted to run the UFWOC by himself without delegating authority. Some people felt Cesar was too demanding. Others criticized him for his arrogance.

In the early 1970s, Cesar Chavez urged people across the country to join him in a second boycott—this time of lettuce.

The union's lettuce boycott spread to the subways of New York City.

There were those who wanted Cesar out of the way no matter what it took. Death threats came in the mail and on the telephone. Were they from growers, angry and bitter for having to meet the demands of their workers and unions? Could the threats come from vengeful Teamster members, carrying grudges over Cesar's efforts to strengthen the UFWOC? More than one person wanted to harm Cesar. His supporters persuaded him to fireproof the new union hall built at Forty Acres outside Delano where he had his office. He also acquired a German shepherd watchdog, which he named Boycott.

At union headquarters outside Delano, Cesar's first guard dog, Boycott, was joined by a second dog named Huelga.

Throughout the 1970s, Cesar continued to lead boycotts and pickets to protest unfair labor conditions.

Despite the dangers, Cesar continued to work for and strengthen the farmworkers' union. In 1972 the AFL-CIO, the powerful national labor federation, granted Cesar's group a special charter. The UFWOC officially became the United Farm Workers, or UFW.

Slowly and steadily, Cesar's efforts won the support of politicians. He campaigned for laws that would make growers maintain safe and clean working conditions. In the summer of 1975, the UFW scored a major victory when California Governor Edmund G. "Jerry" Brown signed the Agricultural Labor Relations Act.

On March 10, 1977, Cesar captured more headlines. After almost ten years of bitter squabbling, he helped patch up differences separating the UFW and the Teamsters. Membership in the UFW grew rapidly. Free from having to compete with the Teamsters, Cesar could focus on helping farmworkers and stopping abuses.

Pesticide use and its possible link to cancer were matters of concern for Cesar Chavez and the United Farm Workers, or UFW, in the 1980s.

In 1980 Cesar's farmworkers' union observed its fifteenth birthday. There was much to celebrate. Hourly pay for members had climbed from less than a dollar to five dollars an hour since 1965. Farmworkers enjoyed medical insurance coverage, unemployment benefits, and pension programs. They also had ways to challenge abuses by employers.

Always concerned about the health and safety of farmworkers, Cesar took an interest in the increased use of pesticides. One study of pesticide use in the mid-1980s was especially troubling. Farmworkers in the San Joaquin Valley of California showed higher than average cancer rates. Scientific studies pointed to sprayed pesticides as the probable cause. Joining consumer advocate Ralph Nader, Cesar urged Americans to stop buying grapes produced on farms where hazardous chemicals were used.

Once more, Cesar turned to fasting as a means to focus attention on the boycott. His doctors disapproved. "Slow down," they urged him. Yet Cesar Chavez would not give in. His people needed him. On July 17, 1988, Cesar stopped eating.

Although there was some media interest in Chavez's fasting, people did not seem as concerned. Times had changed. The public had seen world leaders killed. Wars had cost thousands of American lives. Television and newspapers brought stories of violent crimes into homes every day. The report of one man fasting on behalf of farmworkers did not seem as important as it had years before.

On August 21, 1988, Anthony and Paul Chavez helped their weak and tired father to a chair on a stage platform in Delano. Cesar Chavez sat holding a small wooden cross. Doctors had finally convinced him that he might soon die if he did not end his thirty-six-day-old fast. Nearby stood his wife, Helen, his longtime friend, Ethel Kennedy, and his ninety-six-year-old mother, Juana. Reverend Jesse Jackson, a supporter of human rights activities, moved forward and knelt before Chavez. The frail UFW leader kissed the cross and gave it to Jackson. Jackson promised to carry on the fight.

Cesar Chavez never fully regained his strength after that fast. He continued his work on behalf of the UFW, yet he slowed his pace of activity. His steps were halting, his voice less full. Meetings, speeches, and award ceremonies continued, but Cesar tired quickly. As Cesar's strength diminished, the UFW membership rolls decreased also. From a onetime total of over seventy thousand, memberships slipped to under ten thousand. Cesar bemoaned the situation, but he seemed helpless to do anything about it. "If the union falls apart when I am gone," he said, "I will have been a miserable failure."

In the spring of 1993, Cesar Chavez returned to the place of his birth and childhood near Yuma, Arizona. A large grower who owned property in Arizona and California was suing UFW workers. Cesar was called in to testify for the farmworkers in court.

Visiting the Yuma area brought back many memories to Cesar. The loss of his family's farm during the Great Depression over fifty years before had changed his life.

After his fast in 1988, a weakened Cesar Chavez received support from Reverend Jesse Jackson.

"He felt his family had not been given justice," a friend and coworker recalled. "It hurt him. And he often said it was his first lesson that there is injustice in the world." But it was not Cesar's nature to dwell upon past injustices. Instead, he laid out plans to help farmworkers in the area.

Despite the danger to his health, the UFW leader decided to fast again, seeking to draw attention to the trial.

Newspapers and TV stations recorded Cesar's condition and the courtroom action each day. Many reporters traced Cesar's life, from his modest beginning above his parents' store to his national prominence as a leader for the farmworkers. Some repeated the claims that he was demanding and stubborn.

Staying at the home of a friend, Cesar went to bed early on the night of April 22, 1993. The next morning he was found dead in his room. He was sixty-six years old.

During his life, Cesar Chavez had led many marches, but none was as long as that which followed him in death. In buses and beat-up trucks, by car and on foot, the people came to say good-bye. The crowd numbered some twenty-five thousand in all.

In ninety degree heat, the crowd followed Cesar Chavez's coffin from the heart of Delano to UFW buildings at Forty Acres, a four-mile journey. The mourners carried gladiolas, Helen Chavez's favorite flower, and they lifted red and white banners with the black eagle of the UFW. *"Cesar Chavez—En Nuestras Vidas Para Siempre,"* voices sang out, "Cesar Chavez—In Our Lives Forever."

On a dusty field near the union hall, the people gathered under tents. There were many well-known faces— Ethel Kennedy, Reverend Jesse Jackson, former governor Jerry Brown, and actors Martin Sheen and Edward James Olmos.

Most of the faces, however, belonged to farmworkers— men and women who had stood beside Cesar Chavez in the fields. Together, they had fought for workers' rights.

Mourners gathered near the plain pine casket of Cesar Chavez as his body was carried to UFW headquarters on April 29, 1993.

After the funeral, they would return to lives that had been enriched by the man they had come to honor. Cesar Chavez had been their friend; he had led the way. Now he was gone, but his work would continue. The farm-workers would see to that.

Cesar Chavez, 1927–1993

NOTES

page 7
The term *una causa* has several meanings. Along with the dictionary definition of "a cause," it also meant, to Chavez and his followers, "a community."

page 40
While working for the CSO, Cesar accepted pay adjustments, or raises, but not always without an argument. In 1955, after Chavez rejected one offer, his boss, Saul Alinsky, wrote this response:

". . . For the first time in my association with you I find myself in sharp disagreement with your point of view about
   (a) You do not expect any more adjustments
   (b) That you are being overpaid.
   May I say that in the future there will be adjustments and that you most emphatically are not being overpaid. If you want to have an argument with me on the basis of your convictions in this matter I suggest that you have a talk with your wife first . . . "

page 48
Delano (pronounced dah-LAY-noh) is located in Kern County, California. Before the arrival of Mexican-American workers, including the Chavez family, the area was home to many Chinese-American and Japanese-American workers, as well as "Okies," people who migrated to California from Oklahoma during the dust bowl.

page 57
The Teamsters Union represents workers in transportation and in many other fields. Members include truck drivers, airline stewards, automobile salespeople, soft-drink plant employees, and dairy industry workers.

BIBLIOGRAPHY

Adams, John P. "AFL-CIO Organizers Go After Farm Labor." *Business Week* (September 24, 1960).

Allen, Steve. "Migrant Workers in Your State: Must They Work Dirt Cheap?" *Coronet* (March 1967).

Ball, Charles E. "Farm Labor: What You Can Expect from Union Organizers." *Farm Journal* (May 1972).

Black, Roe C. "The Black Eagle Wins." *Time* (August 10, 1970).

Buckley, William F., Jr. "The Chavez Machine." *National Review* (August 10, 1971).

Chavez, Cesar. "Marcher." *New Yorker* (May 17, 1967).

Chavez, Cesar. "Nonviolence Still Works." *Look* (April 1, 1969).

Chavez, Cesar, and Bayard Rustin. *Right to Work Laws: A Trap for America's Minorities*. New York: A. Philip Randolph Institute, undated.

Coles, Robert. *Migrants, Sharecroppers, Mountaineers*. Boston: Little, Brown and Company, 1971.

Day, Mark. *Forty Acres: Cesar Chavez and the Farm Workers*. New York: Praeger, 1971.

Dunne, John Gregory. *Delano: The Story of the California Grape Strike*. Rev. ed. New York: Farrar, Straus & Giroux, 1971.

Dunning, Harold. *Trade Unions and Migrant Workers: A Worker's Educational Guide*. Washington: International Labour Office, 1985.

Fodell, Beverly. *Cesar Chavez and the United Farm Workers: A Selective Bibliography*. Detroit: Wayne State University Press, 1974.

Fusco, Paul, and George D. Horowitz. *La Causa: The California Grape Strike*. New York: Collier, 1970.

Gates, David. "A Secular Saint of '60s." *Newsweek* (May 3, 1993).

Goodwin, David. *Cesar Chavez: Hope for the People.* New York: Fawcett, 1991.

Grebler, Leo, Joan W. Moore, and Ralph C. Guzman. *The Mexican-American People: The Nation's Second Largest Minority.* New York: The Free Press, 1970.

Henninger, Daniel. "And Now, Lettuce." *New Republic* (October 10, 1970).

Levy, Jacques E. *Cesar Chavez: Autobiography of La Causa.* New York: W. W. Norton & Company, Inc., 1975.

Lindsey, Robert. "Cesar Chavez, 66, Organizer of Union for Migrants, Dies." *New York Times* (April 24, 1993).

London, Joan, and Henry Anderson. *So Shall Ye Reap.* New York: Crowell, 1970.

Matthiessen, Peter. *Sal Si Puedes: Cesar Chavez and the New American Revolution.* Rev. ed. New York: Random House, 1973.

*Rodriguez, Conseulo. *Cesar Chavez.* Philadelphia: Chelsea House Publishers, 1991.

Taft, Philip. *Organized Labor in American History.* New York: Harper & Row, 1964.

Taylor, Ronald B. *Chavez and the Farm Workers.* Boston: Beacon Press, 1975.

Terzian, James P., and Kathryn Cramer. *Mighty Hard Road. The Story of Cesar Chavez.* Garden City, NY: Doubleday, 1970.

Yinger, Winthrop. "Viva La Causa." *Christian Century* (August 27, 1969).

*A star denotes a book for younger readers.
All quotations in this book were taken from the above sources.

INDEX

Cesar Chavez in the late 1970s

Excerpts from *Cesar Chavez: Autobiography of La Causa* by Jacques Levy (New York: W. W. Norton, 1975) appear by permission on pages 11, 15, 20, 22, 27, 31, 34, 35, 37, 43, 44, 48, 51, 64, and 75.

Photographs are reproduced through the courtesy of: Frances M. Roberts, front cover; Archives of Labor and Urban Affairs, Wayne State University, back cover, pp. 7, 13, 18, 28, 33, 38, 42, 46, 50, 56, 59, 62, 65 (bottom), 66; UPI/Bettmann, pp. 2, 49, 54, 60, 63, 65 (top), 68, 71; César E. Chávez Foundation, pp. 8, 10 (both), 12, 20, 21, 22, 24, 25, 79; Library of Congress, p. 14; Wide World Photo, p. 17; West Los Angeles Community Service Organization, p. 30; Associated Press, p. 36; Mickey Pfleger, p. 67; Reuters/Archive Photos, p. 73; United Farm Workers of America, p. 74.